Meandering with Man's Best Friend in Devon.

Chapte

DISCLAIMER

The contents of the book are correct at time of publication. However we cannot be held responsible for any errors or omissions or changes in details or for any consequences of any reliance on the information provided. We have tried to be accurate in the book, but things can change and would be grateful if readers advise me of any inaccuracies they may encounter.

I have taken every care to ensure the walks are safe and achievable by walkers with a reasonable level of fitness. But with outdoor activities there is always a degree of risk involved and the publisher accepts no responsibility for any injury caused to readers while following these walks.

SAFETY FIRST

All the walks have been covered to ensure minimum risk to walkers that follow the routes.

Always be particularly careful if crossing main roads, but remember traffic can also be dangerous even on minor country lanes.

If in the country and around farms be careful of farm machinery and livestock (take care to put dog on lead) and observe the **Country Code**.

Also ensure you wear suitable clothing and footwear, I would advise wearing walking boots which protect from wet feet and add extra ankle support over uneven terrain.

There are a few rules that should be observed if walking alone advise somebody were you are walking and approximate time you will return. Allow plenty of time for the walk especially if it is further and or more difficult than you have walked before. Whatever the distance make sure you have enough daylight hours to complete the walk safely. When walking along a country road always walk on the right to face oncoming traffic, the only exception is on a blind bend were you cross to the left to have a clear view and can be seen from both directions.

If bad weather should come in making visibility difficult, do not panic just try to remember any features along route and get out the map to pinpoint the area but be sure before you move off, that you are moving in the right direction.

Unfortunately accidents can still happen even on the easiest of walks, if this is the case make sure the person in trouble is safe before seeking help. If carrying a mobile phone dial 999 or 112 European Union emergency number will connect you to any network to get you help.

Unmapped walks we recommend that you take the relevant Ordnance Survey map and compass with you, even if you have a Smartphone, digi-walker or G.P.S all of which can fail on route.

Introduction

This book was written to help walkers take your dog out to an area that they just might like to go for a change. It contains ten easy to follow walks all of which are circular and varying in distance from 1.5 miles up to 5.5 miles, so this is anything from a quick stroll or onto something just a bit more testing for you not the dog? The dogs are usually easily pleased with a good run, maybe a few sticks and an area with plenty of sniffs the job is very often done. But we walkers are more demanding we like good views, possibly refreshments along the way with an easy to follow trail with few obstacles nearby.

The walks are all varied from forest, open fields, green lanes, bridleways and quiet country lanes. Most of these walks dogs are able to come off leads and get that extra bit of exercise that they all require. But unfortunately there are some walks where freedom is not so readily available, this could be due to a road or may be livestock in the fields but for whatever reason please be wise to the Country Code.

Remember a dog will ways get excited when you reach and pick-up the lead and they never mind if it is a walk around the block or a route march over the hills. So make the ten circular walks provide a special day out for you and Man's Best Friend out and about together.

Treat the dog walks as a stress relieving exercise because 5 minutes out and about you are totally relaxed, which is then transmitted to the dog. This takes you out into different parts of the countryside and maybe you would like to take a picnic just to make the day last a bit longer. Oh do not forget the ball, or the dog towel sure to be water and that means yes it is time to swim (unless you are a Standard Poodle of course).

We are very lucky in Devon the whole area is very beautiful with many places for dogs to walk and run free, I have tried to keep the stile count down but they are mostly dog friendly. Please always remember the water bottles and dog bowls for a well-earned drink after a great day out in the country.

The walks are different distances so if you have an older dog then take them out on the shorter routes, this makes them feel part of the excitement and fun of a special day for any dog.

Happy Walking.

Meandering with Man's Best Friend in Devon

Chapter 1 Whilborough Common via Kingskerswell Downs

Park & Start Grid ref; SX 874677

Distance: 3 miles

Level; Easy

Time: 1 hour 30 minutes

Terrain: Clear paths on grassland and through wooded areas

Maps. O.S Explorer 110 Torquay to Dawlish

Refreshments Only in Kingskerswell

Amber out on the common.

Great woods for doggy play

Access to start

Leave the A380 and then follow the signpost to Totnes on the A381. Then on entering Two Mile Oak opposite the pub at of the same name, next to the garage turn left onto Whiddon Road. This road further down the line changes name to Maddacombe Road carry straight on under the bridge and up past Foredown Kennels down the slope to reach the car park on the right.

Doggy Things

Vets

Powderham Veterinary Group

7, Powderham Road Newton Abbot Tq12 1EU   telephone; 01626 365119 or

Unit 1 The Willows Village Centre Torquay telephone; 01803 614700.

Chapter 2 Watcombe

Park & Start Grid ref; SX 918673

Distance: 3 miles

Level; Moderate

Time: 2 hour

Terrain: Clear paths on grassland and through wooded areas and down green lanes

Maps. O.S Explorer 110 Torquay to Dawlish

Refreshments Plenty in Torquay

Amber ready for another long walk.

Brunel Woods

Access to start

Take the A380 into Torquay where it changes to A3022 Riviera Way. Then follow through to Lowes Bridge and turn left onto Hele Road A379. Continue on road to the end of Hele Road and again turn left still on A379 but now Teignmouth Road, follow through to road junction and keep left still following A379 Teignmouth Road. Follow road for about 350 metres and take the second turning left onto Moor Lane. Follow for about 100 metres then turn right up Steps Lane to park towards the top.

Doggy Things

Vets

Animal Health Centre

43, Moor Lane Watcombe Torquay TQ2 8NU telephone; 01803 313400

The Walk

(1)

The walk starts towards the top end of Steps Lane past the school on the right to park the car on the road. Then continue on uphill to turn left at the top into Brunel Avenue. Walk down path on far side of road drop down the slope and ignore the first footpath sign to the Teignmouth Road, but carry on down to second sign on the right to Great Hill/Coffinswell which takes you into Brunel Woods.

(2)

Follow the path into the woods up the slight slope for 20 metres and then where the path splits keep over around to the left, then follow the path through a clearing with a collection of Brunel type wooden sculptures on the right, still continue to rise uphill towards Brunel Manor the place that Isambard Kingdom Brunel started to build is Manor House but unfortunately he died before it was finished.

(3)

At the top of the hill with the Brunel Manor straight ahead turn left on the top path and then follow the yellow marked pathway around to the left at the start of a steep climb up hill, this then takes you up high above Watcombe and gives you great views out over Torquay. Carry on along path for almost half a mile to finally emerge out from Brunel Woods onto Seymour Drive, Turn right and start to climb up a steep rise where it soon levels out at the top, the road then drops down slightly stay on path at the end of the road it goes off to the left which is a dead end keep over to the right and follow the path between a white house on the left and Brunel House over the hedge on the right on down to the entrance to Brunel House keep around to the left to follow the road to a junction with the Torquay/Teignmouth Road A379. Cross road carefully and once on the other side turn left to walk 25 metres to the end of the path to turn right down Rock House Lane.

(4)

Then stay on the lane downhill for about half a mile passing the Sladnor Estate on the left to reach a bend in the lane towards the bottom of the lane, on the right at this point there is a green lane signposted half mile to Watcombe. This green lane as the unusual name of Cream Tea Trail so named between the two world wars when families walked from St Marychurch to Maidencombe for their cream teas at Rose Cottage. This lane finally comes into a wooded area but just follow the yellow markers through the woods to emerge out onto the Watcombe Beach Road.

(5)

Turn right at this point, if you went left then this would lead down to Watcombe Beach or the pathway off to Babbacombe. After you turned right then follow lane all the way uphill for a half mile or more to finally reach a road junction with the Torquay/Teignmouth Road A379. Again cross road carefully to enter Moor Lane directly opposite continue down past the school to then turn right into Steps Lane to return to the car parked on the road.

Chapter 3 Coffinswell

Park & Start Grid ref; SX 891685

Distance: 2.5 miles

Level; Moderate

Time: 1 hour 30 minutes

Terrain: Country lanes and down green lanes, ideal for all season walking

Maps. O.S Explorer 110 Torquay to Dawlish

Refreshments Linny Inn.

Amber all ready to read the map?

Out in the countryside

Access to start

Leave M5 motorway at the very end where the road then changes into the A38, then just past the Kennford Services keep over to the left at Telegraph Hill on the A380. Then continue to stay on the A380 for about 10 miles to reach Penn Inn Roundabout at Newton Abbot. Take 2nd exit and continue to follow road on past the Snack Café near the new roundabout. Take first exit and then almost immediately turn left onto Under Way follow lane for about half a mile then bear right into Coffinswell and park near the Linny Pub in the centre of the village.

Doggy Things

Vets

Albany Vets 14, Albany Street Newton Abbot TQ12 2AN telephone; 01626 368000 or

Quarry House Vets 148, Teignmouth Road Torquay telephone; 01803 324341

The Walk

(1)

The walk starts off by parking somewhere near The Linny Inn. Then with The Linny on your left and the small green on the right next to Willowpark Lane follow the lane straight ahead for almost a mile on past the typical Devon high hedges with the magnificent views out over the countryside.

(2)

Then after walking for near on a mile you come into the outskirts of Daccombe carry on past the boundary sign on the right to reach a road junction facing a beautiful thatched cottage at Daccombe Cross. At this point turn left onto Footland Lane and continue to follow the lane up a slope on past a green lane to your left called Downaway Lane.

(3)

Then further up the road where Footland Lane starts to swing around to the right take the little lane off to the left which is Pitland Lane, continue to follow up hill which gets steeper and carries on for about a half mile past horse paddocks and an animal sanctuary about half way up the hill.

(4)

Once at the top of the lane you reach a junction with the main road from Newton Abbot to Torquay, so in the interest of safety do not turn left but turn to the right. Then carefully cross the road to enter Ridge Road only after 10 metres signposted Mount Olive. Continue down lane for about 300 metres ignoring the first turning on the left, but continue on to take the next turning to the left on to a green lane. The green lane is Deerpark Lane just continue around the narrow track finally to pass farm buildings on your left to then reach the main Newton Abbot to Torquay road again.

(5)

Then turn right and carefully cross the busy road, then after only 12 metres turn left down Ridgeway Lane now you start to drop downhill rapidly but be sure to soak up the magnificent views out towards Dartmoor and surrounding area. Now stay on this lane all the way down to the bottom, going past the back of The Linny to then reach the road to Daccombe, turn right here to then return to the parked car.

Chapter 4 Clennon Valley

Park & Start Grid ref; SX 889587

Distance: 2 miles

Level; Easy

Time: 1 hour

Terrain: Lanes and down narrow pathways and open fields around the ponds

Maps. O.S Explorer OL20 South Devon

Refreshments Plenty in Paignton or Goodrington.

Amber is near the beach?

The ponds at Clennon Valley

Access to start

Follow the signpost to Torquay and at the roundabout at the junction of Torquay Road and Riviera Way take 2nd exit onto Hamelin Way. Then at next roundabout take 2nd exit onto Hellevoetsluis Way and then follow road straight through Kings Ash Road to traffic lights at Tweenway Cross. Go straight ahead onto Brixham Road to reach a section of road that widens and at the traffic lights with Premier Inn on the right, turn left onto Goodrington Road, then follow road to almost the end and turn left into Grange Road then after 50 metres turn left and park at Roseland Road.

Doggy Things

Vets

Dart Vale Veterinary Group 31, Manor Road Paignton TQ3 2HZ telephone; 01803 550491

The Walk

(1)

The walk starts off by parking in Grange Road, walk across road to Roseland Road which is now only a pathway signposted Great Fields. This is an easy section to follow just a narrow pathway next to a caravan park that slowly winds up hill which gets steep the further you proceed finally after about a mile reaching the top.

(2)

Once at the top you reach a stile crossover into a field, then cross the field along a well-defined track to a network of paths in a gap between hedge and trees. Go through the gap keeping slightly over to the right and then once through gap turn immediately right with the hedge on your right to follow path as it drops down a steep hill, look out over at this point with views to Goodrington Beach and over Clennon Valley leisure centre sports fields.

(3)

Follow the path downhill to the bottom and into a wooded area soon to see a pond straight ahead. Turn left at the junction and with the pond on your right, then follow path all the way around the pond which as plenty of wildlife on the way. The path then comes out into an open field follow around close to the hedge and take the first turning right which leads between two ponds. Then once you reach the junction where you first turned to go around the first pond turn to the left opposite this path and follow the wide track.

(4)

Then continue to follow the wide track past the large pond on the left which continues on for a fair way, then pass by an information board where the path then starts to narrow. Carry on for about another half mile to reach a small gate, this leads out onto a lane next to the holiday caravan park. Crossover the road carefully and follow the path back around to Roseland Road and onto the car parked in Grange Road.

Chapter 5 Newton Abbot via part of Templer Way

Park & Start Grid ref; SX 871725

Distance: 6 miles

Level; Moderate

Time: 2 hour 45 minutes

Terrain: Teign Estuary Trail, lanes and Templer Way foreshore on Teign Estuary

Maps. O.S Explorer 110 Torquay and Dawlish

Refreshments Plenty in Newton Abbot or at Coombe Cellars Inn.

Amber all ready for long walk.

Teign Estuary looking towards Newton Abbot

Access to start

Come off A380 at Kingsteignton signposted Teignmouth or Newton Abbot Race Course, follow road to traffic lights and turn left before Seymour Horwell garage to park in car park on the left. If this section of path is closed on race day then follow directions below.

Arrive in Newton Abbot and then turn off at the Penn Inn Roundabout take the 3rd exit, then go through the first set of traffic lights then get in lane to turn right at the next set of traffic lights. Once in Brunel Road after traffic lights follow to the end and turn left then follow road around to see the new footbridge over the River Teign straight ahead and park on the road somewhere nearby.

Doggy Things

Vets

Milestone Veterinary Centre Unit 12 Swift Industrial Estate Kingsteignton

Telephone; 01626 362734

The Walk

(1)

The walk starts at Hackney Marshes Nature Reserve car park. Exit car park at the entrance to the road and turn left to follow the path into the Hackney Marshes Nature Reserve. Continue along the path over the first bridge and straight on to cross a small metal bridge and turn right. **N.B. At this point the Teign Estuary Trail may be closed on Newton Abbot Horse Racing Day so check press to be sure.** If all is well then continue along path into Town Quay just over the new footbridge that leads onto Forde Road. Then after just a few metres on this road turn left and follow pavement in the direction of the signs marked Templer Way. Then about 50 metres from the road junction ahead is a Templer Way sign pointing left down a narrow pathway, this goes down the back of two large buildings on your right to reach the River Teign.

(2)

Then follow the track along the side of the River Teign to reach a footbridge over Aller Brook, which forms part of the Aller Brook Nature Reserve which as wildlife like kingfishers and otters. Cross over the Aller Brook via the bridge and then follow the narrow pathway that leads on down under the A380 Newton Abbot bypass to start to walk along the foreshore of the River Teign this is all part of the Templer Way on towards Teignmouth.

N.B. Please remember this walk can only be completed along the foreshore at low tide so observe the instructions on the notices, for your own safety.

If you have timed it correctly then stay on the estuary foreshore which goes around a bay and then crosses a flood wall then on around a wooded section. Continue on in total for about a mile, bear in mind it can be slippery and muddy. But carry on around another small bay and then on past some waterside chalets. Then on that bend straight ahead you will see Coombe Cellars Inn a good watering hole for man and beast.

(3)

If you stopped for refreshments, it is time to retrace your steps back over the flood wall, then leave the Templer Way via a gate on the left if you came back from Coombe Cellars Inn this is right next to the public footpath sign. Go through the gate and then follow the path diagonally across the field on a well-defined track to the top corner. Go through the gateway and continue to follow the track on up to another gateway walk straight through stay on the track to midway through field to reach a large metal gate on your right, next to it is a stile tucked away tight up against the hedge marked with a public footpath sign pointing down the field the way you just came.

(4)

Once over the stile you are out onto a lane turn left on Cross Park Lane which only leads down to Netterton Lodge. Carry on up Cross Park Lane for about 500 metres to the end to reach a road junction. Turn right at the junction and then continue to follow lane for almost a mile on past Manor Cottages and then Manor Farm which is 17th century origin. The lane then starts to climb steadily which you follow for what seems to be miles to finally reach the top of the hill. At this point the lane turns very sharply around a left hand bend, we turn right down a track that is very wide and it only leads down to the estuary foreshore, this was the main access in days gone by to a ferry and ford for crossing the River Teign over to the Passage House Inn on the other side.

(5)

Once you are down the bottom of the track which is a very steep hill, turn left on the foreshore and follow the Templer Way back into Newton Abbot at Town Quay. Then just reverse the outward route back to the car park at Hackney Marshes Nature Reserve.

Chapter 6 Decoy Country Park plus Abbotskerswell

Park & Start Grid ref; SX 866702

Distance: 3 miles

Level; Easy

Time: 2 hour

Terrain: Lake walk, wooded pathways and country lanes.

Maps. O.S Explorer 110 Torquay and Dawlish

Refreshments Decoy Country Park.

Amber thinking what way now?

Decoy Lake.

Access to start

Arrive in Newton Abbot and then turn off at the Penn Inn Roundabout take the 3rd exit, then go to the first set of traffic lights, turn left and through mini roundabout and then under railway bridge to reach another mini roundabout take 3rd exit then after 25 metres turn left into Decoy Country Park.

Doggy Things

Vets

Abbotskerswell Veterinary Centre

The Old Cider Works Abbotskerswell TQ12 5GH telephone; 01626 367972.

The Walk

(1)

The walk starts off from the car park at Decoy Country Park, leave the car park in the direction of the lake and keep around path to the left with the lake on your right. Continue to follow the pathway around the edge of the lake to enter into the woodland area. Carry along this path for about 300 metres to reach a junction. Then at this point turn left and cross a small wooden bridge, then just carry on up the path to reach a large gate at the end which is next to a kissing gate ignoring all other pathways along the way.

(2)

Go through the kissing gate and follow the path through a field before going through another gate and entering the woods to follow the track off to the left. Then just continue along track for about 350 metres to reach a crossroads of paths, turn right here and just a few metres up the track crossover a stile. Once over the stile you are now in a field, follow the path uphill on the outside edge of the woodland to the top corner of the field. Then follow the path around to the left entering in and then out of the woods and up a slope to cross a stile. **N.B Please remember dogs must be on leads if there is livestock in the fields.** Once over the stile and into a field carry on uphill in the direction of the public footpath sign indicates. Then follow the well-defined path through the field finally reaching a stile set back in the hedge at the top of the field.

(3)

Crossover the stile out onto Stoneman Lane, and turn left then follow the lane for a short distance and just past a house with a wooden gate on the right, then keep a lookout for a stile marked with a public footpath sign also on the right. Cross stile and follow the pathway down through the field to come out between two houses onto Laburnum Terrace. Go to the end of Laburnum Terrace and at the road junction turn left onto Manor Road. Then continue to follow Manor Road for about 250 metres to the end and another road junction. Again turn left onto Priory Road and follow lane uphill, then just where the Old Priory High Wall starts and a parking area on the left, you will see a public footpath sign next to a metal gate.

(4)

Go through the gate and follow pathway back through the fields to reach the outskirts of Decoy Country Park, there are different paths from here but all will end up back at the car park in the centre of Decoy Country Park.

Chapter 7 Kingsteignton via Passage House Inn

Park & Start Grid ref; SX 871725

Distance: 2.5 miles

Level; Easy

Time: 1 hour 30 minutes

Terrain: River bank path, open fields, country lanes and old urban streets.

Maps. O.S Explorer 110 Torquay and Dawlish

Refreshments Passage House Inn.

Amber dog in the wild outdoors.

River Teign at Hackney.

Access to Start

Come off the A380 at turning into Kingsteignton signposted to the race course, then follow road through to take 1st exit off mini roundabout. Then at next roundabout take 1st exit again, then at traffic lights turn left just ahead of Seymour Horwell cars, then almost immediately left into car park.

Doggy Things

Vets

Milestone Veterinary Centre Unit 12 Swift Industrial Estate Kingsteignton

Telephone; 01626 362734.

The Walk

(1)

The walk starts at the car park next to the Hackney Marshes Nature Reserve, exit car park via the gate in the corner of car park. Turn right after going through gate and follow the pathway for about 50 metres and then turn left over a small bridge to enter a wooded area. Then carry along the path around to the right ignoring any other pathways to finally reach a gate. Go through the gate and continue to follow the pavement all the way down the back of a housing estate to reach a wide track at the end which is after about 600 metres.

(2)

Turn right onto the wide track and follow the path around the wetland area. This area is a conservation area which you can walk on but please stay on the path and do not mush the marsh, or upset the wildlife. But for the walk then just continue on the track where you rise up a slope and at the top turn left to walk through a tunnel under the railway track. Then take in the magnificent views across the Teign Estuary down towards Teignmouth, then after about half a mile you finally reach the Passage House Inn Complex.

(3)

Then after a visit to the Passage House Inn continue on up the road past the complex up the slope and over the railway bridge, then as you drop down the other side and just before going under the Teignmouth Road A381 bridge turn right up a concrete drive. Then at the top of the drive go through a gate into a large field and keeping to the hedge on left follow the track through the field for about a mile with beautiful views along the way but finally reaching a large gate at the end of the track. Go through gate and take extreme care because this emerges out on to the edge of the Teignmouth Road A381.

(4)

Turn right at the road, and follow the grass verge on up the road then up near the farm buildings carefully close the road, to almost immediately turn left down Coombeshead Road (East). Continue on down the straight lane for just under half a mile, with a barn on the right, turn left at this point up Coombeshead Road and follow for a short distance to the end where it turns into a very narrow pathway. Bear around to the right at the end and then start to rise up a steep slope, at the top you then cross the high footbridge over the A380, which you can use as an observation platform back over the Teign Estuary. Once over the footbridge drop down the other side where you re-join the Coombeshead Road, follow the lane around to the right to reach a road junction. Turn left at road junction still on Coombeshead Road and follow for 50 metres to reach the next road junction onto Longford Lane.

(5)

Turn right onto Longford Lane and also cross the road at this point, then at the second turning left go down Blindwell Avenue and continue to follow for about half a mile to the end to reach the junction of Tarrs Lane. Turn left at this point and follow for just 100 metres to reach junction with Vicarage Hill. Turn right here and then almost immediately before the Dew Drop Inn turn left down Greenhill Road. Stay on the road to reach the 3rd turning right and drop down into Honeywell Road continue to follow to the end where it narrows into a footpath. Cross Prescott Way at the end and then continue on footpath on opposite side of road for about 20 metres then turn left to follow path around to a pedestrian crossing. Cross the road and then enter back in the car park at Hackney Marshes Nature Reserve.

Chapter 8 Galmpton

Park & Start Grid ref; SX 887560

Distance: 2.5 miles

Level; Easy

Time: 1 hour 30 minutes

Terrain: Green lanes, open fields, country lanes.

Maps. O.S Explorer OL20 South Devon

Refreshments Galmpton or Paignton.

Amber's turn to map read today?

Dart Valley Railway line just outside of Greenway Halt

Access to start

Follow the signpost to Torquay and at the roundabout at the junction of Torquay Road and Riviera Way take 2nd exit onto Hamelin Way. Then at next roundabout take 2nd exit onto Hellevoetsluis Way and then follow road straight through Kings Ash Road to traffic lights at Tweenway Cross. Go straight ahead onto Brixham Road to reach a section of road that widens and at the traffic lights with Premier Inn on the right, continue on the A3022 towards Brixham. At the next set of traffic lights turn right still heading to Brixham and take the 2nd turning on right down Greenway Road, continue to follow almost out of village and park on road opposite Greenway Park uphill on the right.

Doggy Things

Vets

Dart Vale Veterinary Group

13/15, Penn Meadow Brixham TQ5 9PW telephone; 01803 862142.

The Walk

(1)

The walk starts at the top of Galmpton village near to Greenway Park, plenty of room to park on road opposite. Then continue to walk uphill past Kennel Lane on the left and then a few metres further on go past Light Lane tucked in on the right next to Galmpton Caravan Park. Then just continue along the country lane which can be busy from time to time with traffic going through to Greenway House follow for about a mile taking in the views and walking parallel with the Dart Valley Railway line for some of the way. Then cast your eye on the higher section out over the trees on the right for a glimpse of the River Dart, then on across a railway bridge to finally reach a road junction off to the left.

(2)

At this point take the road junction off to the left, signposted Maypool and the Youth Hostel. Then climb up the hill along the narrow county lane to the top of the hill to reach two white houses on the right, then turn left onto track opposite if you reach Higher Greenaway Farm you have missed the turning.

(3)

Once on the track follow up a slight rise past houses on the right to reach a small gate on the left. Go through gate and then follow the well-defined pathway uphill through several fields, take your time to look back at the views out over the River Dart. Just continue to stay on the pathway for about a half a mile to reach and enter a small wooded area. Once in the woods and about midway through you come to a junction of pathways, straight ahead will take you on towards Brixham, but we want to turn left onto Coombe Lane which is a narrow green lane that twist and turns all ways through the countryside for about a mile, just carry on to the end of the green lane to reach a junction onto a road.

(4)

Turn left at road junction onto Kennel Lane cross over the railway bridge and follow lane for about 200 metres to the end at another road junction. Turn right and then retrace your steps back into Galmpton village to where the car is parked.

Chapter 9 Haldon Forest via Obelisk

Park & Start Grid ref; SX 905812

Distance: 4 miles

Level; Easy

Time: 2 hour 15 minutes

Terrain: Forest Tracks and country lane.

Maps. O.S Explorer OL44 Torquay and Dawlish

Refreshments None nearby Dawlish or Exeter.

Amber dog free in the forest.

Wide track leading up through the forest.

Access to start

Head for Telegraph Hill and take the A380 towards Newton Abbot, then after about a mile turn left on road signposted Starcross/Mamhead and then almost immediately park on the right avoiding the gateway. If however you are approaching the area from Torquay it is necessary to continue on the A380 in the direction of Telegraph Hill and turn off left to the services, cross over bridge and then re-join the A380 South bound and then follow instructions at the beginning of route.

Doggy Things

Vet

Kingsteignton Veterinary Group

90, Fore Street Chudleigh TQ13 0HT telephone; 01626 853280.

The Walk

(1)

The Walk starts at the layby off the Mamhead Road. Go through the gate onto the forest wide track, and then follow track for about a mile finally reaching a junction of pathways. Turn right and then continue to follow the main track for about a mile and half maybe slightly more ignoring all the other tracks leading off in different directions, these can all be explored the next time you are in the area. **Please** take time to enjoy the views so the dogs can have fun and a good sniff.

(2)

Continue on the track and as you get towards the end starts to rise uphill and at the top you get to see the views out over the coast. Stay on the track but bear in mind that at certain times this track is the huskie exercise route. Once you reach the end of the track you come out on to a road, (leads on) crossover road and into the car park on the opposite side. Go through car park and follow the footpath off to the right and follow the marked trail on down through a wooded area. Towards the end of the wooded area it opens out ahead on to a viewing platform after about 500 metres with the Obelisk just off to the right. Please take your time at the viewing platform and look out over the coastline and on down to the entrance at the Exe Estuary, very important years ago for the wealth of Exeter.

(3)

To carry on the walk continue to follow the way markers as the path bends around in a semi-circle to return back to the car park. Then once back in the car park exit onto the road and turn right, cross road carefully (leads on again) and walk down the grass verge past the first track on the left marked huskie exercise area, and onto the next turning left also marked huskie exercise area but the sign is set back off the road. Now once on the wide track follow all the way downhill to the bottom and at the junction with the main track turn right.

(4)

Follow track for a few metres then turn down left and retrace your steps back to the car in the layby. Job done dogs tried?

Chapter 10 Ashclyst Forest

Park & Start Grid ref; SX 905812

Distance: 2 miles

Level; Easy

Time: 1 hour 15 minutes

Terrain: Forest Tracks and country lane.

Maps. O.S Explorer 115 Exmouth and Sidmouth

Refreshments Killerton House Cafe.

Amber dog at large in Ashclyst Forest.

Amber says great place for us dogs to explore.

Access to start

Leave M5 motorway at junction 29 and then continue on the A3015, turn off right onto Cumberland Way and follow road through to next set of traffic lights. Turn right at traffic lights into Pinhoe and follow road on through Broadclyst. Then after about a mile go past a turning on the left to Killerton and after 100 metres turn right on to narrow lane. Follow lane uphill to park at Deadland parking area on the right.

Doggy Things

Vets

Beaumont Veterinary Centre

31, Main Road Pinhoe EX4 9EY telephone; 01392 460300.

The Walk

(1)

The walk starts from Deadland parking area. This is a very simple walk for the dog owner with maximum fun in my case for Amber dog, plenty to sniff, loads of sticks and may be the odd squirrel. Just leave the car and walk straight ahead up the wide track and then just follow the pathways with the green markers taking you around the wooded areas and into an open grassy area.

(2)

There are other parking areas along the lane, you may not want to climb hills or just keep the walk shorter. So select what is best for you and your dog if time is limited. The experience is great one of total freedom for both man and beast.

More Information on the Meandering Walking Series Paperbacks.

Meandering in Mid Devon
Meandering in South Devon
Meandering on Rivers and Canals in Devon
Meandering Pub Walks in Devon
Meandering Tea Rooms Walks in Devon
Meandering in Gloucestershire
Meandering on the Exe Estuary Trail
Meandering Through History, Mysteries or Legends in Devon
Meandering Pub Walks in Gloucestershire
Meandering with Man's Best Friend in Devon
Meandering the Severn Vale (later in 2016)
Meandering More Pub Walks in Devon (late 2016)

Checkout some of the photos from the Meandering Walking Series

John coombes google plus

Website:

http://johhncoombes.wix.com/meandering-walks-2

Man's Best Friend Amber the Standard Poodle.

Printed in Great Britain
by Amazon.co.uk, Ltd.,
Marston Gate.